EASY

Size

To fit 22- to 23-inch circumference head

Materials

- Medium weight Lion Brand Wool-Ease yarn (197 yds/85g per ball): 1 ball oxford grey #152
- Size 7 (4.5mm) 16-inch circular needle
- Size 8 (5mm) 16-inch circular and double-pointed needles or size needed to obtain gauge
- Stitch marker
- Tapestry needle

Gauge

18 sts and 24 rows = 4 inches/10 cm in St st on larger needles
To save time, take time to check gauge.

Instructions

Hem

Using provisional cast-on (page 14) with smaller circular needle, cast on 92 sts. Place marker to indicate beg of rnd and join, being careful not to twist sts.

Rnds 1–10: Knit.

Rnd 11 (folding ridge): Purl.

Rnds 12–21: Knit.

Next rnd (joining rnd): Fold up hem along folding ridge. Insert RH needle into next st on LH needle and into first st of cast-on round. Knit these 2 sts tog. Continue knitting next st on LH needle tog with next st from cast-on rnd to end of rnd. Remove waste yarn.

Change to larger circular needles.

Knit every rnd until hat measures 7 inches from folding ridge.

Change to double-pointed needles.

Shape Top

Rnd 1: [K2, k2tog] around. (69 sts)

Rnds 2 and 3: Knit.

Rnd 4: [K1, k2tog] around. (46 sts)

Rnds 5 and 6: Knit.

Rnd 7: [K2tog] around. (23 sts)

Rnd 8: K1, [k2 tog] around. (12 sts)

Rnd 9: Rep Rnd 7. (6 sts)

Cut yarn leaving a long end. Weave end through rem sts. Pull tight to close circle. Weave in ends. ∎

Charlie's Hat

INTERMEDIATE

Size

To fit 22- to 23-inch circumference head

Materials

- Medium weight Lion Wool yarn (158 yds/85g per ball): 1 ball each ebony #153 (A) and scarlet #113 (B)
- Size 7 (4.5mm) 16-inch circular needle
- Size 8 (5mm) 16-inch circular and double-pointed needles or size needed to obtain gauge
- Stitch marker
- Tapestry needle

4 MEDIUM

Gauge

18 sts and 24 rows = 4 inches/10 cm in St st on larger needles
To save time, take time to check gauge.

Instructions

Hem

Using provisional cast-on (page 14) and A, with smaller circular needle cast on 92 sts. Place marker on needle to indicate beg of rnd and join, being careful not to twist sts.

Rnds 1–10: With A, knit.

Rnd 11 (folding ridge): Purl.

Rnds 12–21: Knit.

Next rnd (joining rnd): Fold up hem along folding ridge. Insert RH needle into next st on LH needle and into first st of cast-on round. Knit these 2 sts tog. Continue knitting next st on LH needle tog with next st from cast-on round to end of rnd. Remove waste yarn.

Change to larger circular needles.

Knit every rnd until hat measures 3 inches from folding ridge.

[With B knit 2 rnds, with A knit 2 rnds] 3 times.

Continue to knit in rnds with A until hat measures 7 inches from folding ridge.

Change to double-pointed needles.

Shape Top

Rnd 1: [K2, k2tog] around. (69 sts)

Rnds 2 and 3: Knit.

Rnd 4: [K1, k2tog] around. (46 sts)

Rnds 5 and 6: Knit.

Rnd 7: [K2tog] around. (23 sts)

Rnd 8: K1, [k2 tog] around. (12 sts)

Rnd 9: [K2tog] around. (6 sts)

Cut yarn leaving a long end. Weave end through rem sts. Pull tight to close circle. Weave in ends. ∎

Team Support Beanie

INTERMEDIATE

Size

To fit 22- to 23-inch circumference head

Materials

- Medium weight Lion Wool yarn (158 yds/85g per ball): 1 ball each cadet blue #110 (A), scarlet #113 (B) and winter white #099 (C)
- Size 7 (4.5mm) 16-inch circular and double-pointed needles or size needed to obtain gauge
- Stitch marker
- Tapestry needle

Gauge

21 sts and 30 rows = 4 inches/10 cm in Pat st
To save time, take time to check gauge.

Pattern Stitch

Rnds 1–3: *K2, p2; rep from * around.
Rnd 4: Knit.
Rnd 5: Purl.
Rnd 6: Knit.

Instructions

With circular needle and A, loosely cast on 88 sts. Place marker on needle to indicate beg of rnd and join, being careful not to twist sts.

Rnds 1–3: [K2, p2] around.
Rnd 4: With B, knit.
Rnd 5: Purl.
Rnd 6: With C, knit.
Rnds 7–9: [K2, p2] around.
Rnd 10: With A, knit.
Rnd 11: Purl.
Rnd 12: With B, knit.
Rnds 13–15: [K2, p2] around.
Rnd 16: With C, knit.

Rnd 17: Purl.
Rnd 18: With A, knit.
Rep Rnds 1–18.
Rep Rnds 1–11. Cut A and C.
Change to double-pointed needles.

Shape Top

With B, knit 1 rnd.
Rnd 1: [K2tog, p2tog] around. (44 sts)
Rnd 2: [K1, p1] around.
Rnd 3: [Ssk] around. (22 sts)
Rnd 4: [K2tog] around. (11 sts)
Cut yarn leaving a long end. Weave end through rem sts. Pull tight to close circle. Weave in ends. ∎

Nothing But Ribbing Beanie

EASY

Size

To fit 22- to 23-inch circumference head

Materials

- Medium weight Lion Brand Wool-Ease yarn (162 yds/70g per ball): 1 ball autumn #233
- Size 8 (5mm) 16-inch circular and double-pointed needles or size needed to obtain gauge
- Stitch marker
- Tapestry needle

4 MEDIUM

Gauge

24 sts and 24 rows = 4 inches/10 cm in k1, p1 rib slightly stretched
To save time, take time to check gauge.

Instructions

With circular needles, loosely cast on 96 sts. Place marker on needle to indicate beg of rnd and join, being careful not to twist sts.

Rnd 1: *K1, p1; rep from * around.

Rep Rnd 1 until hat measures 7 inches from beg.

Change to double-pointed needles.

Shape Top

Rnd 1: *K1, p1, k1, p2tog, k2tog, p1; rep from * around. (72 sts)

Rnds 2–4: *K1, p1; rep from * around.

Rnd 5: *Ssk, p2tog, k1, p1; rep from * around. (48 sts)

Rnds 6–8: *K1, p1; rep from * around.

Rnd 9: *P2tog, ssk; rep from * around. (24 sts)

Rnd 10: *P1, k1; rep from * around.

Rnd 11: *K2tog; rep from * around. (12 sts)

Cut yarn leaving a long end. Weave end through rem sts. Pull tight to close circle. Weave in ends. ∎

Many-Colored Beanie

INTERMEDIATE

Size

To fit 22- to 23-inch circumference head

Materials

- Medium weight Patons Classic Merino Wool yarn (223 yds/100g per ball): 1 ball each that's blue #77134 (A), burgundy #00208 (B), black #00226 (C) and leaf green #00240 (D)
- Size 7 (4.5mm) 16-inch circular and double-pointed needles or size needed to obtain gauge
- Stitch marker
- Tapestry needle

4 MEDIUM

Gauge

20 sts and 28 rows = 4 inches/10 cm in St st
To save time, take time to check gauge.

Pattern Note

Slip all sts as to purl unless otherwise stated.

Instructions

With circular needles and A cast on 96 sts. Place marker on needle to indicate beg of rnd and join, being careful not to twist sts.

Rnd 1: Purl.

Rnd 2: Knit.

Rnd 3: Purl.

Rnd 4: With B, [k1, sl 1] around.

Rnd 5: [P1, sl 1 wyib] around.

Rnd 6: With A, knit.

Rnds 7–9: Rep Rnds 1–3.

Rnds 10–12: With B, knit.

Rnd 13: With C, knit.

Rnd 14: Purl.

Rnds 15–17: With B, knit.

Rnd 18: With D, [k3, sl 1] around.

Rnd 19: [P3, sl 1 wyib] around.

Rnds 20–24: Rep Rnds 10–14.

Rnds 25–26: With B, knit.

Rnd 27: With A, [k1, sl 1] around.

Rnds 28 and 29: Knit.

Rnd 30: With C, [sl 1, k1] around.

Rnds 31: Knit.

Change to double-pointed needles.

Shape Top

Rnd 1: [K6, k2tog] around. (84 sts)

Rnd 2: Knit.

Rnd 3: [K5, k2tog] around. (72 sts)

Rnd 4: With D, knit.

Rnd 5: [K4, k2tog] around. (60 sts)

Rnd 6: Knit.

Rnd 7: With C, [k3, k2tog] around. (48 sts)

Rnd 8: Knit.

Rnd 9: [K2, k2tog] around. (36 sts)

Rnd 10: Knit.

Rnd 11: [K1, k2tog] around. (24 sts)

Rnd 12: [K2tog] around. (12 sts)

Rnd 13: Rep Rnd 12. (6 sts)

Cut yarn leaving a long end. Weave end through rem sts. Pull tight to close circle. Weave in ends. ■

EASY

Size

To fit 22- to 23-inch circumference head

Materials

- Medium weight Patons Classic Merino Wool yarn (197 yds/85g per skein): 1 ball each russet #00206 (A) and old gold #00204 (B)
- Size 7 (4.5mm) 16-inch circular needle
- Size 8 (5mm) 16-inch circular and double-pointed needles or size needed to obtain gauge
- Stitch marker
- Tapestry needle

Gauge

18 sts and 24 rows = 4 inches/10 cm in St st on larger needles
To save time, take time to check gauge.

Instructions

Hem

Using provisional cast-on, page 14, with smaller circular needles and A, cast on 92 sts. Place marker on needle to indicate beg of rnd and join, being careful not to twist sts.

Rnds 1–10: Knit.

Rnd 11 (folding ridge): Purl.

Rnds 12–21: With B, knit.

Next rnd (joining rnd): Fold up hem along folding ridge. Insert RH needle into next st on LH needle and into first st of cast-on rnd. Knit these 2 sts tog. Continue knitting next st on LH needle tog with next st from cast-on rnd to end of rnd. Remove waste yarn.

Change to larger circular needles and A.

Knit every rnd until hat measures 7 inches from folding ridge.

Change to double-pointed needles.

Shape Top

Rnd 1: [K2, k2tog] around. (69 sts)

Rnds 2 and 3: Knit.

Rnd 4: [K1, k2tog] around. (46 sts)

Rnds 5 and 6: Knit.

Rnd 7: [K2tog] around. (23 sts)

Rnd 8: K1, [k2 tog] around. (12 sts)

Rnd 9: Rep Rnd 7. (6 sts)

Cut yarn leaving a long end. Weave end through rem sts. Pull tight to close circle. Weave in ends. ∎

A Bit of Tweed Beanie

INTERMEDIATE

Size
To fit 22- to 23-inch circumference head

Materials
- Medium weight Patons Classic Merino Wool yarn (223 yds/100g per ball): 1 ball each new denim #77115 (A) and denim marl #77116 (B)
- Size 7 (4.5mm) 16-inch circular needle
- Size 8 (5mm) 16-inch circular and double-pointed needles or size needed to obtain gauge
- Stitch marker
- Tapestry needle

4 MEDIUM

Gauge
18 sts and 24 rows = 4 inches/10 cm in St st on larger needles
To save time, take time to check gauge.

Instructions

Hem
Using provisional cast-on (page 14) with smaller circular needles and A, cast on 92 sts. Place marker on needle to indicate beg of rnd and join, being careful not to twist sts.

Rnds 1–10: Knit.

Rnd 11 (folding ridge): Purl.

Rnds 12–21: With B, knit.

Next rnd (joining rnd): Fold up hem along folding ridge. Insert RH needle into next st on LH needle and into first st of cast-on round. Knit these 2 sts tog. Continue knitting next st on LH needle tog with next st from cast-on rnd to end of rnd. Remove waste yarn.

Change to larger circular needles.

*With A, knit 10 rnds.

With B, knit 10 rnds.

Rep from * until hat measures 7 inches from fold line.

Continuing in stripe pat as established, change to double-pointed needles.

Shape Top
Rnd 1: [K2, k2tog] around. (69 sts)

Rnds 2 and 3: Knit.

Rnd 4: [K1, k2tog] around. (46 sts)

Rnds 5 and 6: Knit.

Rnd 7: [K2tog] around. (23 sts)

Rnd 8: K1, [k2 tog] around. (12 sts)

Rnd 9: Rep Rnd 7. (6 sts)

Cut yarn leaving a long end. Weave end through rem sts. Pull tight to close circle. Weave in ends. ∎

Pull-Top Beanie

EASY

Size
To fit 22- to 23-inch circumference head

Materials
- Bulky weight Lion Brand Wool-Ease Chunky yarn (153 yds/140g per ball): 1 ball each spice #135 (A) and walnut #127 (B)
- Size 10.5 (6.5mm) 16-inch circular needle or size needed to obtain gauge
- Stitch marker

5
BULKY

Gauge
13 sts and 19 rows = 4 inches/10 cm in St st
To save time, take time to check gauge.

Special Abbreviation

M1 (make 1):
Inc 1 by inserting LH needle from front to back under horizontal thread between st just worked and next st, knit into the back loop.

Instructions
With A, loosely cast on 57 sts. Place marker on needle to indicate beg of rnd and join, being careful not to twist sts.

Rnd 1: Purl.

Rnd 2: Knit.

Rnd 3: Purl.

Rnd 4: With B, k1, [M1, k11] 5 times, k1. (62 sts)

Rnds 5–7: Knit.

Rnd 8: With A, k1 [k2tog, k10] 5 times, k1. (57 sts)

Rnds 9–12: Rep Rnds 1–4.
Knit every rnd until hat measures 7 inches from beg.

Shape top
Rnd 1: With A, k1, [k2tog, k8] 6 times, k1. (56 sts)

Rnd 2: Purl.

Rnd 3: [K6, k2tog] 7 times. (49 sts)

Rnd 4: Purl.

Rnd 5: K2, [k2tog, k5] 5 times, k2tog, k3. (42 sts)

Rnd 6: Purl.

Rnd 7 (eyelet rnd): [K4, yo, k2tog] 7 times.

Rnd 8: Purl.

Rnd 9: Knit.

Rnd 10: Purl.

Rnds 11 and 12: Rep Rnds 9 and 10.
Bind off.

Finishing
Twisted Cord
Cut 2 strands of B, each 60 inches long. Tie ends to a door handle or hook. Twist the strands counterclockwise until yarn twists up on itself when relaxed. Hold yarn at middle of twisted strand, remove end from handle and allow yarn to twist onto itself. Cut Twisted Cord 18-inches long. Tie overhand knot 1½ inches from each end. Thread cord through eyelets, beginning and ending in same opening. Pull ends of cord to gather top and tie into a knot. ■

A Touch of Brim Beanie

INTERMEDIATE

Size

To fit 22- to 23-inch circumference head

Materials

- Medium weight Lion Wool yarn (223 yds/100g per ball): 1 ball each midnight blue #111 (A) and pumpkin #133 (B)
- Size 8 (5mm) 16-inch circular and double-pointed needles or size needed to obtain gauge
- Stitch markers (different colors)
- Tapestry needle

4 MEDIUM

Gauge

18 sts and 24 rows = 4 inches/10 cm in St st
To save time, take time to check gauge.

Special Abbreviation

W/T (wrap & turn):

On a knit row:

Sl next st purlwise, bring yarn to front between needles, sl the same st back to LH needle. Turn, move yarn to back between needles in preparation for purling. (One stitch is wrapped.)

On a purl row:

Sl next st purlwise, move yarn to back between needles, sl the same st back to LH needle. Turn, bring yarn to front between needles in preparation for knitting. (One stitch is wrapped.)

Knit wrap and stitch together:

When short row-shaping is completed, pick up each wrapped st by inserting RH needle under the wrap and into the wrapped st, knit them tog.

Instructions

Hem

Using provisional cast-on (page 14) and A, cast on 92 sts. Place marker on needle to indicate beg of rnd and join, being careful not to twist sts.

Rnds 1–8: Knit.

Rnd 9: K45, place marker, knit to end.

For short-row shaping: K43, W/T; p41, W/T; k40, W/T; p39, W/T; k38, W/T; p37, W/T; k36, W/T; p35, W/T.

Next rnd: Knit all sts, knitting wrap and wrapped st tog.

Next rnd (folding ridge): Purl.

Note: The 2nd half of short-row shaping is intentionally shorter than the first half.

For short-row shaping: K41 W/T; p37, W/T; k38, W/T; p39, W/T; k40, W/T; p41, W/T.

Next rnd: Knit to end of rnd knitting wrap and wrapped st tog.

Knit 9 rnds even.

Next rnd (joining rnd): Fold up hem along folding ridge. Insert RH needle into next st on LH needle and into first st of cast-on rnd. Knit these 2 sts tog. Continue knitting next st on LH needle tog with next st from cast-on rnd to end of rnd. Remove waste yarn.

Knit 3 rnds, removing marker for brim.

Beg Stripe Pattern

Rnd 1: With B, knit.

Rnd 2: With A, knit.

Rnds 3 and 4: Rep Rnds 1 and 2.

Row 5: With B, knit

Rnds 6–9: Rep Rnds 1 and 2.

Rnd 10: With B, knit.

Change to double-pointed needles and A.

Shape Top

Rnd 1: [K2, k2tog] around. (69 sts)

Rnds 2 and 3: Knit.

Rnd 4: [K1, k2tog] around. (46 sts)

Rnds 5 and 6: Knit.

Rnd 7: [K2tog] around. (23 sts)

Rnd 8: K1, [k2 tog] around. (12 sts)

Rnd 9: Rep Rnd 7. (6 sts)

Cut yarn leaving a long end. Weave end through rem sts. Pull tight to close circle.

Finishing

Fold brim out and up toward joining rnd. Sew through four layers of fabric ¼ inch from fold. ■

Windowpanes of Color Beanie

INTERMEDIATE

Size

To fit 22- to 23-inch circumference head

Materials

- Medium weight Patons Classic Merino Wool yarn (223 yds/100g per ball): 1 ball each dark grey mix #00225 (A), paprika #00238 (B), that's purple #77330 (C) and leaf green #00240 (D)
- Size 7 (4.5mm) 16-inch circular and double-pointed needles or size needed to obtain gauge
- Stitch marker
- Tapestry needle

Gauge

20 sts and 32 rows = 4 inch/10 cm in Pat st
To save time, take time to check gauge.

Pattern Stitch

Windowpane Stripe

Rnd 1: With A, knit.

Rnd 2: Purl.

Rnds 3 and 4: With B, [k3, sl 1] around.

Rnds 5 and 6: With A, rep Rnds 1 and 2.

Rnds 7 and 8: With D, rep Rnds 3 and 4.

Rnds 9 and 10: With A, rep Rnds 1 and 2.

Rnds 11 and 12: With C, rep Rnds 3 and 4.

Rep Rnds 1–12 for pat.

Pattern Note

Slip all sts as to purl unless otherwise stated.

Instructions

With circular needles and A cast on 96 sts. Place marker to indicate beg of rnd and join, being careful not to twist sts.

Rnd 1: Purl.

Rnd 2: With B, [k3, sl 1] around.

Rnd 3: [P3, sl 1 wyib] around.

Rnd 4: With A, knit.

Rnd 5: Purl.

Rnd 6: With C, [k1, sl 1, k2] around.

Rnd 7: [P1, sl 1 wyib, p2] around.

Rnd 8: With A, knit.

Rnd 9: Purl.

Rnds 10 and 11: With D, rep Rnd 2.

Rnds 12 and 13: With B, rep Rnds 6 and 7.

Rnds 14 and 15: With C, rep Rnd 2.

Work [Rnds 1–12 of Windowpane Stripe pat] twice.

Work Rnds 1–6 of Windowpane Stripe pat.

Change to double-pointed needles.

Shape Top

Rnd 1: With D, knit.

Rnd 2: [K4, ssk] around. (80 sts)

Rnd 3: With A, knit.

Rnd 4: Purl.

Rnd 5: With C, knit.

Rnd 6: [K3, k2tog] around. (64 sts)

Rnd 7: With A, knit.

Rnd 8: Purl.

Rnd 9: With B, knit.

Rnd 10: [K2, ssk] around. (48 sts)

Rnd 11: With A, knit.

Rnd 12: [P1, p2tog] around. (32 sts)

Rnd 13: With D, knit.

Rnd 14: [K2tog] around. (16 sts)

Rnd 15: With A, knit.

Rnd 16: [P2tog] around. (8 sts)

Cut yarn leaving a long end. Weave end through rem sts. Pull tight to close circle. Weave in ends. ∎

Ear-Warming Cables Beanie

EASY

Size

To fit 22- to 23-inch circumference head

Materials

- Bulky weight Lion Brand Wool-Ease Chunky yarn (153 yds/140g per ball): 1 ball grass #130
- Size 10.5 (6.5mm) 16-inch circular and double-pointed needles or size needed to obtain gauge
- Stitch marker
- Cable needle (cn)
- Stitch holder
- Tapestry needle

5
BULKY

Gauge

18 sts and 22 rows = 4 inches/10 cm in Pat st
To save time, take time to check gauge.

Special Abbreviations

C4B (cable 4 back):

SI next 2 sts onto cn and hold in back, k2, k2 from cn.

C5B (cable 5 back):

SI next 2 sts onto cn and hold in back, k3, k2 from cn.

C6B (cable 6 back):

SI next 3 sts onto cn and hold in back, k3, k3 from cn.

Inc (increase):

Inc 1 by knitting in the front and back of the next st.

M1 (make 1):

Inc 1 by inserting LH needle from front to back under horizontal thread between st just worked and next st, knit into the back loop.

Stitch Pattern

Rnd 1: [P4, k6] around.

Rnd 2: Knit.

Rnds 3 and 4: Rep Rnds 1 and 2.

Rnd 5: Rep Rnd 1.

Rnd 6: [K4, C6B] around.

Instructions

Earflap

With circular needle, cast on 10 sts.

Row 1 (WS): K2, p6, k2.

Row 2: Inc, k7, inc, k1. (12 sts)

Row 3: K3, p6, k3.

Row 4: K3, C6B, k3.

Row 5: Rep Row 3.

Row 6: Inc, k9, inc, k1. (14 sts)

Row 7: K4, p6, k4.

Row 8: Knit.

Rows 9 and 10: Rep Rows 7 and 8.

Row 11: Rep Row 7.

Row 12: K4, C6B, k4.

Rows 13–16: [Rep Rows 7 and 8] twice.

Row 17: K4, p6, k4.

Place these 14 sts on holder.

Rep for 2nd earflap leaving sts on needle.

Next rnd (joining rnd): Knit across 14 earflap sts, cast on 23 sts, knit 14 earflap sts from holder, cast on 23 sts. (74 sts)

Place marker on needle to indicate beg of rnd and join being careful not to twist sts.

Rnd 1: *P4, k6, [p4, k5] 3 times; rep from * around.

Rnd 2: Knit.

Rnd 3: Rep Rnd 1.

Rnd 4: *K4, C6B, [k4, sl next 2 sts to cn and hold in back, k3, (k1, M1, k1) from cn] 3 times; rep from * once. (80 sts)

Beg Stitch Pattern and work even until hat measures 5 inches from joining rnd, ending with Rnd 4 of Stitch Pattern.

Change to double-pointed needles.

Shape Top

Rnd 1: [P1, p2tog, p1, k2, k2tog; k2] around. (64 sts)

Rnd 2: [K3, C5B] around.

Rnd 3: *[P3, k5] around.

Rnd 4: Knit.

Rnds 5 and 6: Rep Rnds 3 and 4.

Rnd 7: [P1, p2tog; k2, k2tog, k1] around. (48 sts)

Rnd 8: [K2, C4B] around.

Rnd 9: [P2, k4] around.

Rnd 10: Knit.

Rnd 11: *P2tog, [k2tog] twice; rep from * around. (24 sts)

Rnd 12: Knit.

Rnd 13: [P1, k2tog] around. (16 sts)

Rnd 14: [K2tog] around. (8 sts)

Cut yarn leaving a long end. Weave end through rem sts. Pull tight to close circle. Weave in ends. ■

INTERMEDIATE

Size
To fit 22- to 23-inch circumference head

Materials
- Medium weight Lion Brand Wool-Ease yarn (197 yds /85g per ball): 1 ball each peacock #170 (A), cranberry #138 (B), black #153 (C), gold #171 (D) and purple #147 (E)
- Size 7 (4.5mm) 16-inch circular and double-pointed needles or size needed to obtain gauge
- Stitch marker
- Stitch holder
- Tapestry needle

Gauge
20 sts and 28 rows = 4 inches/10 cm in St st
To save time, take time to check gauge.

Special Abbreviation

M1 (make 1):

Inc 1 by inserting LH needle from front to back under horizontal thread between st just worked and next st, knit into the back loop.

Pattern Note
Slip all sts as if to purl unless otherwise stated.

Instructions
With circular needles and A, loosely cast on 88 sts. Place marker on needle to indicate beg of rnd and join, being careful not to twist sts.

Rnd 1: Purl.

Rnd 2: With B, knit.

Rnd 3: Purl.

Rnds 4 and 5: Rep Rnds 2 and 3.

Rnd 6: With A, knit.

Rnd 7: Purl.

Rnd 8: With C, knit.

Rnds 9 and 10: With D, [k3, sl 1] around.

Rnds 11 and 12: With C, [k1, sl 1, k2] around.

Rnds 13 and 14: With C, rep Rnds 9 and 10.

Rnd 15: With E, knit.

Rnd 16: Purl.

Rnd 17: With D, [k1, sl 1] around.

Rnd 18: With B, [p1, sl 1 wyib] around.

Rnds 19 and 20: With E, rep Rnds 15 and 16.

Rnds 21–23: With B, knit.

Rnd 24: With C, knit.

Rnd 25: Purl.

Rnds 26–28: With A, knit.

Rnds 29 and 30: With B, rep Rnds 24 and 25.

Rnds 31–33: With D, knit.

Rnds 34 and 35: With B, rep Rnds 24 and 25.

Rnds 36–38: With E, knit.

Rnds 39 and 40: With B, rep Rnds 24 and 25.

Change to double-pointed needles.

Shape Top
Rnd 1: With B, knit.

Rnd 2: [K6, k2tog] around. (77 sts)

Rnd 3: With A, knit.

Rnd 4: [K5, k2tog] around. (66 sts)

Rnd 5: With D, knit.

Rnd 6: [K4, k2tog] around. (55 sts)

Rnd 7: With E, knit.

Rnd 8: [K3, k2tog] around. (44 sts)

Rnd 9: With B, knit.

Rnd 10: [K2, k2tog] around. (33 sts)

Rnd 11: With A, knit.

Rnd 12: [K1, k2tog] around. (22 sts)

Rnd 13: With D, knit.

Rnd 14: [K2tog] around. (11 sts)

Rnd 15: With C, knit.

Rnd 16: Purl.

Cut C, leaving a 6-inch length.

I-Cord Top-Knots

With double-pointed needle and E, k4, place rem 7 sts on holder. *K4, slide sts to other end of needle; rep from * until I-cord measures 3 inches. [K2 tog] twice, bind off. Cut yarn and pull end through rem st.

Place next 4 sts on double-pointed needle. Join A and make a 2nd I-cord in same manner.

Place last 3 sts on double-pointed needle. Join B, k1, M1, k1. Make 3rd I-cord in same manner on these 4 sts.

Finishing

With C length, sew across opening at base of I-cords. Weave in ends. Tie each I-cord into an overhand knot. ∎

Provisional Cast-On

To work this type of cast-on, start with a crochet chain one or two stitches longer than the number of stitches to be cast on for the pattern you are working. Since this chain is removed, it is best to make it with a contrasting color.

Once the chain is completed, with knitting needle, pick up and knit in the back bump of each chain (Photo 1) until the required number of stitches is on the needle. Continue to work the pattern as given in the instructions.

To join cast-on stitches with "live stitches" on the needle, insert right-hand needle into next stitch on left-hand needle and into the corresponding stitch on the cast-on round (Photo 2). Knit these two stitches together. Continue in this manner until all stitches are joined.

Remove waste yarn and complete hat as indicated in instructions.

Photo 1

Photo 2

Abbreviations & Symbols

approx	approximately	rnd(s)	rounds
beg	begin/beginning	RS	right side
CC	contrasting color	skp	slip, knit, pass stitch over; one stitch decreased
ch	chain stitch	sk2p	slip 1, knit 2 together, pass slip stitch
cm	centimeter(s)		over the knit 2 together; 2 stitches have been decreased
cn	cable needle	sl	slip
dec	decrease/decreases/decreasing	sl 1k	slip 1 knitwise
dpn(s)	double-pointed needle(s)	sl 1p	slip 1 purlwise
g	gram	sl st	slip stitch(es)
inc	increase/increases/increasing	ssk	slip, slip, knit these 2 stitches together; a decrease
k	knit	st(s)	stitch(es)
k2tog	knit 2 stitches together	St st	stockinette stitch/stocking stitch
LH	left hand	tbl	through back loop(s)
lp(s)	loop(s)	tog	together
m	meter(s)	WS	wrong side
M1	make one stitch	wyib	with yarn in back
MC	main color	wyif	with yarn in front
mm	millimeter(s)	yd(s)	yard(s)
oz	ounce(s)	yfwd	yarn forward
p	purl	yo	yarn over
pat(s)	pattern(s)		
p2tog	purl 2 stitches together		
psso	pass slipped stitch over		
p2sso	pass 2 slipped stitches over		
rem	remain/remaining		
rep	repeat(s)		
rev St st	reverse stockinette stitch		
RH	right hand		

[ ] work instructions within brackets as many times as directed

( ) work instructions within parentheses in the place directed

** repeat instructions following the asterisks as directed

* repeat instructions following the single asterisk as directed

" inch(es)

How to Check Gauge

A correct stitch-gauge is very important. Please take the time to work a stitch gauge swatch about 4 x 4 inches. Measure the swatch. If the number of stitches and rows are fewer than indicated under "Gauge" in the pattern, your needles are too large. Try another swatch with smaller-size needles. If the number of stitches and rows are more than indicated under "Gauge" in the pattern, your needles are too small. Try another swatch with larger-size needles.

Skill Levels

BEGINNER
Beginner projects for first-time knitters using basic stitches. Minimal shaping.

EASY
Easy projects using basic stitches, repetitive stitch patterns, simple color changes and simple shaping and finishing.

INTERMEDIATE
Intermediate projects with a variety of stitches, mid-level shaping and finishing.

EXPERIENCED
Experienced projects using advanced techniques and stitches, detailed shaping and refined finishing.

Metric Charts

INCHES INTO MILLIMETERS & CENTIMETERS (Rounded off slightly)

inches	mm	cm	inches	cm	inches	cm	inches	cm
1/8	3	0.3	5	12.5	21	53.5	38	96.5
1/4	6	0.6	5 1/2	14	22	56	39	99
3/8	10	1	6	15	23	58.5	40	101.5
1/2	13	1.3	7	18	24	61	41	104
5/8	15	1.5	8	20.5	25	63.5	42	106.5
3/4	20	2	9	23	26	66	43	109
7/8	22	2.2	10	25.5	27	68.5	44	112
1	25	2.5	11	28	28	71	45	114.5
1 1/4	32	3.2	12	30.5	29	73.5	46	117
1 1/2	38	3.8	13	33	30	76	47	119.5
1 3/4	45	4.5	14	35.5	31	79	48	122
2	50	5	15	38	32	81.5	49	124.5
2 1/2	65	6.5	16	40.5	33	84	50	127
3	75	7.5	17	43	34	86.5		
3 1/2	90	9	18	46	35	89		
4	100	10	19	48.5	36	91.5		
4 1/2	115	11.5	20	51	37	94		

KNITTING NEEDLE CONVERSION CHART

U.S.	1	2	3	4	5	6	7	8	9	10	10 1/2	11	13	15	17	19	35	50
Continental-mm	2.25	2.75	3.25	3.5	3.75	4	4.5	5	5.5	6	6.5	8	9	10	12.75	15	19	25

The designer of these beanies wishes to dedicate this book to
Charlie, my favorite guy, who helped with the design variations.

American School of Needlework ®
excellence in instruction

DRG Publishing
306 East Parr Road
Berne, IN 46711
©2006 American School of Needlework

TOLL-FREE ORDER LINE or to request a free catalog (800) 582-6643
Customer Service (800) 282-6643, **Fax** (800) 882-6643

Visit AnniesAttic.com.

ISBN: 978-1-59012-180-1   All rights reserved.   Printed in USA   8, 9, 10, 11, 12, 13, 14